How Your Pet Gro

Gipper the Guinea Pig

Jane Burton

Random House New York

 Published in the United States by Random House, Inc., New York, and simultaneously in Canada by Random House of Canada Limited, Toronto.

Library of Congress Cataloging in Publication Data: Burton, Jane. Gipper the guinea pig. (How your pet grows!)
SUMMARY: Photographs and text follow a guinea pig and his siblings as they grow, learn, and play during their first year of life. 1. Guinea pigs—Juvenile literature. 2. Guinea pigs—Development—Juvenile literature. 3. Guinea pigs as pets—Juvenile literature. [1. Guinea pigs] I. Title. II. Series. SF459.G9B87 1988 636′.93234 88-3253
ISBN: 0-394-89961-X (pbk.); 0-394-99961-4 (lib. bdg.)

Manufactured in Hong Kong 1 2 3 4 5 6 7 8 9 0

With thanks to Fiona Hatchell and Katie MacDonald for all their help

Puzzle the guinea pig is about to become a mother. Her belly is big and round.

During the night, Gipper and his four sisters are born. Puzzle licks the limp and drowsy piglets clean. Soon Gipper opens his eyes and tries to sit up—but not for long. He joins his sisters for a drink of Puzzle's milk, and then they snuggle around her for a rest.

Three hours old

Gipper's fur has dried, and he is warm and safe. Puzzle leaves her babies in a sleepy huddle while she goes off to eat. The hard work of giving birth has made her hungry.

One day old

Gipper is wide-eyed and alert. He was born with teeth and can already nibble grass.

Gipper has a "crest" just like Puzzle's—a circle of white fur on the top of his head. The white hairs spread out from the center like the petals of a daisy.

Two days old

Baby guinea pigs can scamper soon after birth. On this sunny day Gipper and his sisters follow their mother outside. The piglets move along with jerky little steps as they call “*Tut-tut! Tut-tut!*” to each other.

Puzzle is "mowing" her way across another part of the lawn, chomping on the tasty grass. Soon the piglets miss her. Their quiet *"tuts"* turn into loud squeaks—*"Week! Week! Weeek!"* Puzzle returns, chirruping softly to her babies.

Seven days old

Guinea piglets nibble solid food but cannot eat much of it. At seven days old they still depend on their mother's milk.

Puzzle has five babies but only two teats. The piglets have to take turns drinking her milk. When several piglets crowd underneath her all at once, Puzzle is nearly lifted off the ground!

Gipper and his sister Flora are nibbling on grass. Gipper takes some into his mouth, tugs and pulls, and nearly does a headstand before the grass stem breaks and he can eat it. The piglets mutter and chuckle all the time. But at any sudden noise, they get very quiet and prick up their ears to listen. Soon, if all is well, everyone is munching and muttering again.

The piglets often stop to clean themselves. Gipper likes to scratch with a hind foot and rub his face with both paws. Flora can twist around and reach her back.

They are playful, too. They love to hop, skip, and make sudden little jumps. And when they are tired, like Gipper is now, they stop and rest. Soon the piglets will cuddle close to Puzzle and go to sleep.

Three weeks old

Guinea pigs hate to get wet. On rainy days they stay indoors, munching grass and waiting for the sun to shine again.

Four weeks old

Three young rabbits are grazing nearby. They are the same age as Gipper but twice as big. A rabbit can sit up taller than a guinea pig, and see farther too. But Gipper can do something the rabbits cannot do—he can squeak when they bump into him.

Eight weeks old

The guinea pigs are itching and might scratch until their fur comes out. They need a medicated bath to stop the itching. Everyone hates the water and complains loudly. Flora and Gipper try to scramble away.

After his bath Gipper is drenched. He rears up and spin-dries himself. The drops fly out in a shower, leaving him damp. Soon he will be dry and glossy again.

Ten weeks old

Ginger the kitten is lapping milk from a bowl. He is so busy, he does not see Gipper coming near. Ginger is so startled that he jumps up and lands in the milk! Now there is milk all over the floor—and all over Ginger, too.

The piglets need a second bath to stop their itching. Ginger is sticky and wet from the milk, so he has a bath too. Later they all snuggle down in a nest of warm towels.

Three months old

Gipper meets a longhair guinea pig named Ruffle. He puts his nose in the air to sniff the stranger. Ruffle sniffs back. They walk around each other cautiously, waddling on stiff legs and rocking from side to side. Gipper makes an unfriendly sound. Ruffle puts his front feet on Gipper's back. This makes Gipper squeak. But instead of fighting, they go their separate ways.

Five months old

Gipper's sister Daisy has three babies of her own. As she cleans Goldie, her firstborn, Goldie combs her face with the claws of a hind foot. She twists around and licks her fur. She even licks Scruffy, her brother. Gipper is fascinated by the new arrivals and their strange smells. He comes over to take a look.

Daisy's instinct to protect her babies—even from Gipper—is very strong. She lunges with her mouth open and jabs with her teeth. Gipper says *"Week!"* in surprise. He and Daisy are tooth-to-tooth, but they do not bite. Gipper goes away muttering.

Six months old

How Gipper's family has grown! Puzzle has had five more babies, and each of Gipper's sisters has had two or three. Gipper's brothers and sisters and nieces and nephews are everywhere. There are twenty guinea pigs in all.

Seven months old

Gipper and his nephew Scruffy are scampering among the early fall apples. Gipper stops and puts his nose in the air, sniffing the other guinea pigs who are out enjoying the sunshine.

Eight months old

Crisp autumn leaves are scattered on the grass. Gipper and his own crested daughters, Petal and Sepal, are grazing. There is no need for a lawn mower with so many guinea pigs around!

Soon the flowers will die and the weather will turn cold. Gipper and his family will spend the winter indoors, munching on sweet, dry hay until grass begins to grow again in the spring.